IMAGES
of America

CLEVELAND'S
LAKE VIEW CEMETERY

LAKE VIEW ANGEL. The cemetery is famous for Victorian angels like this one that keeps guard over the Morse family burial plot. The angel's dramatic wings and trumpet indicate that it is of the next world, but its face is strikingly human. The monument symbolizes the close connections between death and life that characterize the cemetery. (Roy Woda.)

IMAGES
of America

CLEVELAND'S
LAKE VIEW CEMETERY

Marian J. Morton

ARCADIA
PUBLISHING

Published by Arcadia Publishing
Charleston, South Carolina

Library of Congress Catalog Card Number: 2003114540

For all general information contact Arcadia Publishing at:
Telephone 843-853-2070
Fax 843-853-0044
E-mail sales@arcadiapublishing.com
For customer service and orders:
Toll-Free 1-888-313-2665

Visit us on the Internet at www.arcadiapublishing.com

ART AND THE NATURAL LANDSCAPE. Lake View founders believed that in a rural cemetery, artful monuments would enhance and complement nature. These graceful mausoleums built into the hillside and surrounded by mature trees prove the founders right. (James W. Garrett IV.)

CONTENTS

ACKNOWLEDGMENTS

Without the help of the Lake View Cemetery staff, this book would not have been possible. I want to thank especially these people: President and Chief Executive Officer William L. Garrison for lending me photographs from Lake View's archives; Corporate Secretary and Director of Community Relations Mary C. Krohmer for her hospitality; Memorial Adviser Laura Roberts Dempsey for her splendid photographs and expert advice; and all of the people who have kept Lake View the most beautiful place in which I have ever worked.

Thanks also to John Carroll University for generous financial support; Michael J. Johns of Johns-Carabelli Company Mayfair Memorials for sharing his expertise about monuments, many of which his company has created over the last century; Dr. John J. Grabowski of the Western Reserve Historical Society for kind assistance with photographs from his library and Anne Salcich of the Western Reserve Historical Society for finding them; Roy Woda for again lending me his extraordinary photographs; and most especially to James W. Garrett IV for his cheerful company, his never-failing inspiration, and his amazing photographs.

Finally, I want to dedicate this book to the memory of my grandparents, who are buried at Lake View: Mr. and Mrs. Richard Inglis and Mr. and Mrs. David L. Johnson.

INTRODUCTION

Since 1869, Lake View Cemetery has shaped and shared the fortunes of the city of Cleveland. Lake View was the city's first rural cemetery, an escape from the pollution and congestion of a swiftly urbanizing Cleveland, bcoming a model for the city's parks and suburbs. At Lake View are buried men and women who built lasting monuments to themselves there and in Cleveland. They were joined by tens of thousands of others whose lives shaped the city and the cemetery in less visible but equally important ways. Today Lake View is no longer an isolated rural retreat, but it remains a vital part of the communities it has helped to create.

From 1860 to 1870, Cleveland's population more than doubled, reaching 92,829. The Civil War hastened the city's industrialization; Cleveland's iron and steel foundries and oil refineries flourished. Thousands of newcomers from nearby towns and distant European villages found work in Cleveland. Some made their fortunes. Among them was Jeptha H. Wade, who was born in Seneca County, New York. A man of many talents and interests, Wade built telegraph lines across the Midwest; his company was absorbed into Western Union Telegraph in 1856, the year Wade came to Cleveland. He became the first president of Lake View.

Wade and other cemetery founders, proud of their prospering city, believed that Cleveland should have a rural, or garden, cemetery like Boston's Mount Auburn or Cincinnati's Spring Grove. The city of Cleveland and surrounding townships already maintained cemeteries, as did the Cleveland Catholic Diocese and several Protestant and Jewish congregations. Established in the first decades of the nineteenth century, these cemeteries looked much like their urban neighborhoods. Their modest stone monuments and headstones were generally arranged on a formal grid, resembling the layout of city streets. By the post-Civil War years, some of these older cemeteries, surrounded by commerce or industry, were in disrepair.

In contrast, rural cemeteries like Lake View were created on the outskirts of cities on sites with dramatic natural landscapes that could be enhanced by curved roadways, artful plantings, and carefully designed monuments. Such cemeteries—their founders hoped—would reconnect urban dwellers with the beauty and healing qualities of nature, console mourners, inspire visitors, and encourage pride in the local and national past.

Most of Lake View's first trustees lived on Euclid Avenue, known in the post-Civil War era as "Millionaires' Row." When they looked for a site for the new cemetery, they naturally looked east up the avenue. They found their spot in East Cleveland Township, six miles from Cleveland's Public Square. The area, known as "Smith Run," consisted of several properties on a ridge that extended from Mayfield (State) Road north to Euclid. Picturesque streams and ravines ran north and south through the ridge, which at its highest point was 175–200 feet above Lake Erie with a splendid view of the lake. Eventually Lake View included 285 acres, bounded on the west by Little Italy, on the north by Euclid and Forest Hill Avenues, on the east by Coventry and Superior Roads, and on the south by Mayfield. Imposing entrances were built on both Euclid and Mayfield.

As Lake View trustees had recognized, Cleveland's boundaries and population were moving east. In East Cleveland Township, the villages of Collamer, Collinwood, and Glenville were becoming summer residences to some of Cleveland's wealthy families. Several of the cemetery's early trustees owned, or would soon own, property near Lake View in the neighborhood that is today University Circle. They assumed that their property values would be enhanced by the presence of this scenic, park-like cemetery. In 1874, Wade himself owned considerable property in this area. So did trustees Dr. Worthy S. Streator and Liberty S. Holden, publisher of the *Cleveland Plain Dealer*. John D. Rockefeller, already on his way to becoming the world's richest man, had bought a summer home in East Cleveland Township, just east of the cemetery. He joined the Lake View board of trustees in 1878. He and his family would acquire 700 acres in the vicinity, becoming major players in suburban real estate.

In 1882, Wade boosted both civic pride and the value of his real estate by donating to the city of Cleveland, 64 acres of property, which became the city's first large public park. Named after its donor, Wade Park adjoined the elegant subdivision laid out by Wade and later developed by his grandson, Jeptha H. Wade Jr. The subdivision lay between East 105th and East 115th Streets from East Boulevard to Ashbury Avenue and included Wade Park Avenue and Magnolia Drive. In 1896, Wade Park became a vital link in Cleveland's developing park system, which began at the Shaker Lakes, ran west along the Doan Brook watershed, through Wade Park and Rockefeller Park to Gordon Park on Lake Erie. Just to the east of Wade Park, Lake View's lawns and trees complemented both the park system and Wade's residential development nearby.

Lake View Cemetery was non-sectarian although in the nineteenth century, "non-sectarian" generally meant "Protestant." The cemetery was open to all, but its distance from the city and the cost of its grave sites, especially compared to those in public cemeteries, meant that its initial clientele was at least middle-class. Trustees in fact hoped that Lake View would attract "the best citizens of Cleveland." And it did. The trustees themselves—including Wade, Holden, Streator, as well as lawyer and leading Democrat Henry B. Payne, businessman and philanthropist Joseph Perkins, industrialist Moses C. Younglove, and Republican activist and banker William Bingham—purchased family burial plots.

In 1881, Lake View became the burial place of the assassinated President James Abram Garfield, and in 1890, a permanent, much grander monument was built to memorialize the fallen president. This monument much enhanced the cemetery's national and local prestige. The streetcars that reached the Euclid Avenue gate and in 1890, the Mayfield gate, made the cemetery accessible to the public. Lake View became such a popular a recreation spot that on Sundays only visitors with tickets could be admitted.

Frequent Sunday visitors, however, did not prevent the cemetery from experiencing financial difficulties during the 1890s, as did Cleveland and the rest of the nation. The trustees in 1892 considered establishing some less expensive lots "within reach of persons of moderate means." Lake View fell into a "neglected, farm-like condition . . . [T]he roads were unimproved, the lawns uneven and uncultivated, . . . [T]he whole physical condition deplorable, and [the cemetery] was financially discredited," admitted a trustees' report two decades later.

Nevertheless, by the turn of the twentieth century, the presence of Lake View had fostered the growth of three neighboring communities, in addition to University Circle. Just to the west of the cemetery was Little Italy in Cleveland. It became home to the stone cutters and gardeners who created the cemetery's monuments and maintained its grounds. The northern section of the cemetery fell within the suburb of East Cleveland, established in 1895 as an extension of Millionaires' Row, east on Euclid, and the location of Rockefeller's summer home. Lake View was East Cleveland's only park. Its mayor, Charles E. Bolton boasted in 1901 of the cemetery's "high terraced land, cut by beautiful ravines. . . . On knoll, bank, and terrace, under ornamental shade and beneath fragrant shrubs, lie thousands of citizens of the lake metropolis

[Cleveland]." The southernmost portion of the cemetery became part of Cleveland Heights after the suburb was founded in 1901. According to local legend, the view from the top of the Garfield Monument had inspired Cleveland Heights' first large developer, Patrick Calhoun, to plan his prestigious Euclid Heights allotment just to the south of the cemetery in the 1890s. Boston landscape designer E.W. Bowditch, who also designed Cleveland's park system, laid out curving streets for Calhoun's allotment that were much like the pathways he laid out in the cemetery. The streetcar soon extended past the cemetery gate east on Mayfield, further encouraging Cleveland Heights' development.

East Cleveland and Cleveland Heights grew rapidly during the 1920s when Cleveland's middle class began to leave the city, their departure facilitated first by the streetcar and then by the automobile. Cleveland Heights families who owned plots in the cemetery got special keys to the Mayfield gate. Lake View's population and popularity kept pace with this growth. The cemetery purchased adjoining properties in Little Italy and raised the price of a single grave from $60 to $75.

The Great Depression, however, brought hard times. Payments on cemetery plots purchased during the affluent twenties became difficult to collect; the cemetery threatened to "remove bodies to a single grave section and resell the lot" if debts were not paid. Some financially strapped customers had to sell back parts of their family plots. Maintenance workers and grave diggers took a cut in hourly wages (except for those who made less than 55¢ an hour); ten men were laid off. Those still on the payroll unionized, joining a local chapter of the Arborists and Landscapers in 1938.

Prosperity returned to the country and the cemetery after the United States entered World War II. Lake View supported the war effort by lending land for victory gardens. But made cautious by the recent brush with financial catastrophe, the Lake View management again resolved to aim its "advertising and sales efforts at the man of moderate means . . . [rather] than relying on large sales to people in the higher income brackets, which are becoming scarcer each month." The price of a single grave went back down to $60. The war-induced labor shortage, along with the union, created new difficulties. In 1947, the union went on strike for a 10¢ an hour raise as the cost of living skyrocketed. The strike made local headlines, as unburied caskets piled up. Three men, one a Methodist minister, crossed the picket line to dig their mother's grave themselves. After almost three months, the strike ended when the union accepted a 4¢ an hour raise. Lake View continued to have labor difficulties: workers went on strike in 1973, 1976, 1980, and 1993.

During the 1950s and 1960s, Lake View listed record numbers of interments. But national trends were unsettling. The 1963 publication of Jessica Mitford's *The American Way of Death*, a merciless expose of the commercialization of the funeral industry, prompted many to replace the traditional burial (and burial plot) with cremation. More ominously, there were signs of trouble close to home. Urban renewal had destroyed Cleveland homes and neighborhoods. Racial tensions culminated in destructive riots in 1966 and 1968. Cleveland's population began a steep decline as its industrial base weakened, and whites and African Americans fled to neighboring suburbs.

During the 1960s and 1970s, African-American families moved into East Cleveland and Cleveland Heights. White families from these suburbs, Lake View's previously predominant clientele, moved east or south. There was increased competition from public and sectarian cemeteries farther from Cleveland. Potential customers worried that Lake View was in a dangerous neighborhood. In 1965 cemetery trustees briefly considered buying property in Gates Mills.

By 1981, the Garfield Monument had fallen into disrepair. The National Park Service and private donors came to the rescue, and the renovated monument was rededicated in 1985. But the physical decline of the monument, combined with decline in interments, suggested that Lake View might go the way of the old, urban cemeteries that it had supplanted. In response, the cemetery administration initiated several community outreach efforts. These stressed Lake View's two greatest assets: history and horticulture. Both received considerable attention in the cemetery's quarterly newsletter, *The Heritage,* first published in 1986. Advertising also capitalized on Lake View's claim to house the historically significant. "Impress Your Relatives

When They Come to Visit. You'll have your own place in history, along with President James A. Garfield [and] financier John D. Rockefeller. . . . There's room for you," or "Save a Place in History, Before You're History," urged the Lake View brochures.

Walking tours, trolley rides, and special events of both national and local interest now attract hundreds of thousands of visitors to Lake View every year. Cemetery officials hope that some will come back and stay permanently.

This story of Lake View is also the story of Cleveland. Lake View remains the final resting place of the founders and leaders of many of Cleveland's oldest political, cultural, and economic institutions. Today, Lake View's population also includes the newer residents of Cleveland and the neighboring suburbs. Diversity in class, religion, and ethnicity has altered the Lake View landscape, as have changing ideas about remembering life and death. Now in the heart of Cleveland communities, Lake View continues to enliven and enrich the lives of its visitors and neighbors.

One

THE CEMETERY AND THE CITY

LAKE VIEW TODAY. This map illustrates the curvilinear paths and planned ponds typical of a nineteenth-century rural cemetery. These were intended to enhance the natural landscape and differentiate the rural cemetery from the grid plan of urban streets. The map also illustrates that the city now surrounds the cemetery. (Lake View Cemetery.)

JEPTHA H. WADE'S HOME. Lake View founder Wade lived at 3917 Euclid Avenue, Cleveland's "Millionaires' Row," pictured here in 1874. His Italianate villa was surrounded by elaborate gardens. Lake View Cemetery also reflected this interest in landscaping. (Western Reserve Historical Society.)

WADE PROPERTY IN UNIVERSITY CIRCLE. This 1874 atlas shows Wade's properties in what is here called "Euclid Avenue Park." Euclid Avenue appears as the southern boundary. Doan Street is now East 105th Street. Wade's plan for a residential allotment and his donations of some of this property for a public park and the Cleveland Museum of Art helped to develop University Circle as Cleveland's cultural center. (Western Reserve Historical Society.)

ERIE STREET CEMETERY, 1900. This public burial place was established by the City of Cleveland in 1826. By 1900, the cemetery was in the center of a busy commercial district. The iron fence, similar to the one that enclosed Wade's Euclid Avenue home, was forbidden at Lake View because fences interrupted the view of the landscape. (Lake View Cemetery.)

EAST CLEVELAND CEMETERY, 1900. Founded by East Cleveland Township in 1849 and almost directly across Euclid Avenue from Lake View, this simple public cemetery was the burial place of many of the township's founding families. As in the Erie Street Cemetery, plots were small, and headstones and monuments were close together. The cities of East Cleveland and Cleveland Heights share responsibility for the maintenance of this cemetery, and it has often been neglected. (Lake View Cemetery.)

13

EUCLID AVENUE, c. 1900. Like Wade, many of Lake View's early trustees lived on Euclid Avenue. This "showplace of America" was home to Cleveland's most successful industrialists, merchants, and professionals. Many of them moved east up the avenue and re-created their elegant neighborhood in Lake View. (*Picturesque Cleveland.*)

ROCKEFELLER PARK, c. 1900. This park was donated by John D. Rockefeller to the City of Cleveland in 1896, on the occasion of the city's centennial. As at Lake View, the roadway (now Martin Luther King Boulevard) curves along the water, Doan Brook, down to Lake Erie. The park is the site of Cleveland's Cultural Gardens and the city's greenhouse. (*Picturesque Cleveland.*)

14

LAKE VIEW OFFICE.
This first small office on Euclid Avenue could be reached initially by the horse-drawn streetcar and then the electric streetcar that continued east to the East Cleveland Township villages of Collamer, Collinwood, and Glenville. These were becoming summer residences for Cleveland's well-to-do families. (Lake View Cemetery.)

LONDON ILLUSTRATED NEWS. When the cemetery became the burial place of President James Abram Garfield in 1881, Lake View gained international recognition. This is the artist's rendering, not an accurate representation of the cemetery. Note the curving paths and artistically arranged monuments. The inset is the Garfield vault, which would be replaced in 1890 by the Garfield Monument. (Western Reserve Historical Society.)

15

FUNERAL, 1900. A burial at Lake View could be a grand social event, as indicated by the banks of flowers, the formal awning, and the large crowd at this somber funeral for a family that died in a boating accident. (Lake View Cemetery.)

LAKE VIEW, 1906. The cemetery became a favorite subject for postcards. The view looks south to the Garfield monument through one of the more crowded sections of the cemetery in which headstones and monuments of varying sizes and shapes create a visually pleasing diversity. All monuments, however, had to be approved by Lake View's board of trustees. (Lake View Cemetery.)

Lake View Cemetery, seen from Garfield Memorial, CLEVELAND, OHIO.

THE VIEW OF THE LAKE, 1907. Lake View's site on a ridge high above the city of Cleveland was chosen because of the drama of its natural landscape. The densely wooded land rises sharply to the south until it is 175–200 feet above the lake. This postcard of the view from the top of the Garfield Monument shows the lake to the northwest and the distant smokestacks of the industrial city that cemetery founders helped to build. Much of the cemetery remained undeveloped although some very significant monuments had already been built. (Special Collections, Cleveland State University.)

EUCLID AVENUE, 1915. By this time, commerce had begun to move up Euclid Avenue across from Lake View's gates. Farther east along the streetcar tracks lay the new suburb of East Cleveland. (Lake View Cemetery.)

EUCLID AVENUE GATE. This imposing gate and the iron fence separated the cemetery from the encroaching city. The gate was created in 1924 by the architectural firm of Hubbell and Benes, which had earlier designed the Wade Chapel at Lake View, the Cleveland Museum of Art, and the West Side Market, among other Cleveland landmarks. (Lake View Cemetery.)

EUCLID HEIGHTS, c. 1900. Developer Patrick Calhoun planned this exclusive allotment across Mayfield to the south of Lake View in Cleveland Heights. One of several grand mansions on Overlook Road, the home in the foreground is now the site of Waldorf Towers; the home in the distance still stands. Many of the residents of this elite development, including the owners of these two homes, are buried at Lake View. (*Picturesque Cleveland.*)

MAYFIELD GATE. This simple wooden gate and fence initially guarded the Mayfield Road entrance. The walls on this south side of the cemetery had not yet been built. The cemetery obviously enjoyed cordial relations with its Cleveland Heights neighbors. (Lake View Cemetery.)

NEW MAYFIELD GATES. In 1940, landscape designer A.D. Taylor presented to the Lake View board of trustees his plan for these handsome stone pillars and decorative iron gates. This was not yet considered the cemetery's main entrance. Funeral processions were more likely to enter through the Euclid Avenue gates. However, as Cleveland's population moved east and south from the city, the Mayfield entrance, completed in 1941, became more convenient. Taylor worked for Lake View intermittently through the 1930s as the cemetery's straitened budget allowed. He was responsible for the redesign of the lake behind the Wade Chapel. A plaque on one of the pillars notes that Lake View is on the National Register of Historic Places. (Lake View Cemetery.)

FOREST HILL PARK, 1938. A.D. Taylor also laid out Cumberland Park in Cleveland Heights and Forest Hill Park in East Cleveland and Cleveland Heights. The parkland, formerly John D. Rockefeller's estate, was donated to the two suburbs by John D. Rockefeller Jr. A portion of the park was just across Superior Road from Lake View. Taylor's plan utilized the ponds, carefully arranged plantings, and curving pathways characteristic of rural cemeteries. (Case Western Reserve University Special Collections.)

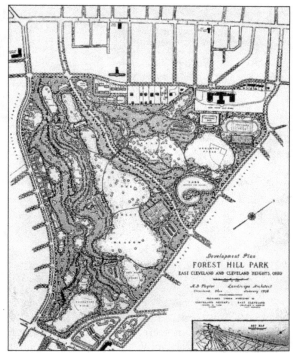

LAKE VIEW LANDSCAPE, 1941. The woods, lawns, and decorative hedges of Lake View's garden setting were deliberately different from older cemeteries and provided a model for parks such as Forest Hill as well as for the landscaping of suburban homes. In this section of the cemetery, monuments and headstones are uniformly set back from the roadway, much as suburban houses are from the street. (Lake View Cemetery.)

FAMILY PLOT. A plot such as this, surrounded by trees and shrubs and provided with a bench, gave privacy for the family in this place of public grandeur. A plot and a monument also promised that the family name would be preserved for posterity. (Lake View Cemetery.)

LAKE VIEW, 1955. This aerial view shows that the wooded cemetery serves as a park in the now densely settled area. Mayfield Road is in the right-hand corner of the photograph. Just north of Mayfield is the Garfield Monument. The Wade Chapel's roof is visible through the trees on the lower left. (Lake View Cemetery.)

VIEW FROM THE TOP, 1962. The view to the northwest from the top of the Garfield Monument shows the continued eastward expansion of the city, indicated by the new buildings at University Circle and the homes of Little Italy. (Lake View Cemetery.)

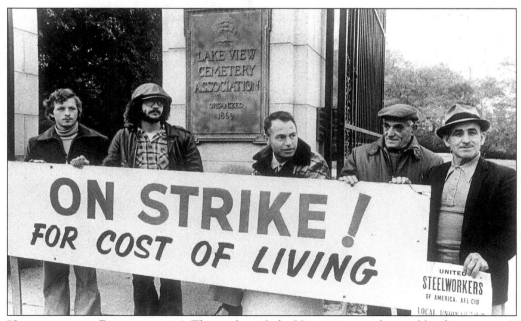

VIEW FROM THE BOTTOM, 1976. This strike at Lake View was one of several by the cemetery's employees after they unionized in 1938. The pickets asked for a "cost of living" raise for the cemetery's grave diggers and maintenance men. (Lake View Cemetery.)

THE CEMETERY AND THE CITY TODAY. The view west from the top of the Garfield Monument still shows Lake Erie and smoke stacks in the far distance, just as in the 1907 postcard on page 17. But above the lake looms Cleveland's dramatically changed downtown skyline. Closer are the new high-rise buildings of University Circle and the homes and Holy Rosary Church of Little Italy. The camera reveals the changed spatial connections between the city and the cemetery: the urban landscape has come closer and closer to the rural cemetery in the decades since its founding. These connections between the city and the cemetery have been strengthened by their shared past and present. (Lake View Cemetery.)

Two

FOUNDERS AND LEADERS

JEPTHA HOMER WADE (1811–1890). The founder and first president of Lake View Cemetery was a banker, financier, horticulturist, artist, and philanthropist. Like many men and women buried at Lake View, Wade became a civic leader, serving on the city's park commission, as director of the city workhouse, and on the boards of many private institutions and corporations. (Western Reserve Historical Society.)

WADE MONUMENT. At the highest point of the cemetery, with an unimpeded view of Lake Erie and the city, stands this dramatic monument to Lake View's founder Jeptha Homer Wade. Nearby are buried Wade's son Randall (1835–1876), and his grandson Jeptha H. Wade Jr. (1857–1926), who shared many of his grandfather's interests, especially in Lake View. The winged angel at the top of the pedestal adds to the monument's height and suggests the final triumph of eternal life over death. When he founded Lake View in 1869, Wade correctly guessed that Cleveland's population would move east. He could not have predicted the smokestacks on the lake shore that now echo his monument's verticality. (James W. Garrett IV.)

WADE PARK LAGOON, JULY 4, 1888. This graceful pond was created on the parkland donated by Wade to the city of Cleveland in 1882. The lagoon became a popular recreation spot. Band concerts were staged on the banks of the lagoon, and boating facilities were provided. In the distance to the right was the first Cleveland zoo, to which Wade gave a herd of deer. The zoo also housed two black bears, two wild cats, two foxes, birds, and other animals. As homes and cultural institutions were built in the Wade Park neighborhood, the zoo was moved to Brookside Park and became part of the Cleveland Metroparks system. The striking fountain, finished in 1886 at a cost of $1,500, was referred to as the "Horse Fountain" or "Man on a Horse." It has now disappeared. The Fine Arts Garden compensates for this loss. (Western Reserve Historical Society.)

WADE CHAPEL, c. 1901. Jeptha Homer Wade Jr. donated this mortuary chapel to the cemetery in memory of his grandfather. The architectural firm of Hubbell and Benes designed the classical temple, a style shared by many of the cemetery's family mausoleums. The building, which opened in 1901, is listed on the National Register of Historic Places. (*Picturesque Cleveland.*)

WADE CHAPEL INTERIOR. The lavish windows and mosaics were created by the studio of Louis Comfort Tiffany, who also did many of the windows of the smaller mausoleums. The walls depict the artist's conception of "the journey of life." The central window, a detail of which is seen here, presents the Christian promise of eternal life. (Lake View Cemetery.)

CLEVELAND MUSEUM OF ART, 1917. The museum stands in the park donated by Jeptha Homer Wade, a portion of which had been set aside for an art museum. Bequests from three other Cleveland businessmen—Hinman B. Hurlburt, Horace Kelley, and John Huntington—made the museum possible. Hubbell and Benes were the architects of the neo-classical building. Jeptha H. Wade Jr. donated much of his personal collection to the museum. Opened in 1916, it has always been free to the public. The museum overlooks the Wade Park Lagoon and the Fine Arts Garden. (Western Reserve Historical Society.)

JAMES ABRAM GARFIELD (1831–1881). Garfield was born in a log cabin in Orange Township in Cuyahoga County. His father died when Garfield was two years old, and his mother supported the family with difficulty. Garfield later commented that he did not recommend poverty. He went to work at age 13, but managed to attend the Western Reserve Eclectic Institute (later Hiram College) and to graduate from Williams College in 1856. He returned to Hiram to teach classics and served as the college's president from 1858 until 1861. In 1859, he was elected to the Ohio Senate. He served with distinction in the Union Army during the Civil War until 1863 when he was elected to the U.S. House of Representatives. In 1880, Garfield was elected to the U.S. Senate, but received the Republican nomination for president before he could serve. He was a compromise candidate between warring factions of the Republican Party, his candidacy doubtless aided by the fact that he was from Ohio, a politically pivotal state during this period. (Lake View Cemetery.)

GARFIELD CATAFALQUE. Garfield was shot only four months after taking office and died in September 1881. Much mourned by a public that remembered the assassination of President Abraham Lincoln, Garfield lay in state under this funeral canopy in Cleveland's Public Square, as Lincoln had only 16 years earlier. (Lake View Cemetery.)

LAKE VIEW ARCH. This postcard pictures the temporary arch placed at the entrance to Lake View for Garfield's funeral. "Come Home to Rest," welcomed the sign to this president, who had lived nearby in Mentor. Garfield was also an ordained minister of the Disciples of Christ. (Lake View Cemetery.)

FIRST VAULT. The assassinated president was temporarily entombed in this handsome Romanesque vault at Lake View where services were held and thousands of mourners were received. (Lake View Cemetery.)

HONOR GUARD. Garfield's body was guarded by a regiment of Civil War veterans before its entombment. Garfield's successful command of the 42nd Ohio Regiment was a political asset. (Lake View Cemetery.)

GARFIELD MONUMENT. After Garfield's death, the Garfield National Monument Association raised $135,000 from states and private individuals for this grander burial place, which became Lake View's signature structure. In 1890, on Memorial Day, the monument was dedicated in a ceremony attended by President Benjamin Harrison, former President Rutherford B. Hayes, and future President William McKinley. The architect, George Keller, combined Romanesque, Byzantine, and Gothic styles. The monument is a circular tower of Ohio sandstone, 50 feet in diameter and 180-feet high that can be seen for miles around. Broad steps lead up to the porch that surrounds the structure, and they often serve as a stage for public events. (Lake View Cemetery.)

MONUMENT PANEL. Five bas-relief panels depicting Garfield's life and death encircle the base of the monument. This panel portrays Garfield the orator. The more than 100 figures on the panels are life-size. The monument is actually a mausoleum, combining the tomb and memorial functions since Garfield and his wife Lucretia are buried here. (Lake View Cemetery.)

INTERIOR STATUE. Inside the monument is this life-size Carrara marble statue of Garfield, striking a pose similar to the one in the frieze. The sculptor was Alexander Doyle. The statue stands underneath a mosaic dome; stained glass windows represent the 13 original colonies and Ohio. The Garfield National Monument Association donated the monument to the cemetery in 1923. In 1985, the monument was refurbished with funds from the National Park Service and private contributors. (Lake View Cemetery.)

HENRY CHISHOLM (1822–1881). This commanding statue of Chisholm, almost a contemporary of Garfield's, stands opposite the Euclid Avenue gates and marks Chisolm's burial site. The relief below the figure depicts men working in the mills. The back of the monument reads: "Erected by 6,000 Employees and Friends in Memory of Henry Chisholm, Christian Philanthropist and Everyone's Friend." (James W. Garrett IV.)

CLEVELAND ROLLING MILLS. Chisholm was a founder of these mills on Cleveland's south side, which specialized in making iron and steel parts. Heavy industry became the basis of the Cleveland economy in the last decades of the nineteenth century and provided jobs for hundreds of thousands of European immigrants. After Chisholm's death, his mills became the scene of violent, but unsuccessful strikes by workers of several nationalities. Cleveland Rolling Mills was eventually absorbed into U.S. Steel. (Western Reserve Historical Society.)

ROUSE MONUMENT. Benjamin Rouse (1795–1871) and his wife Rebecca (1799–1887) arrived in Cleveland in 1830. He had left a successful career as a real-estate developer in New York City to become an agent for the American Sunday School Union. He spent years organizing Sunday schools in the Western Reserve area, testimony to the lively sectarianism of the period. He and his wife were founders of First Baptist Church and leaders of the city's religious and charitable activities. The inscription under the sculpture reads: "And now abide faith, hope, and charity," referring to the three classical bronze figures above, as well as to the Rouses' religiously inspired work. The draped urn symbolizes mourning. (James W. Garrett IV.)

REBECCA CROMWELL ROUSE. She single-handedly directed several charitable organizations: the Martha Washington and Dorcas Society, which distributed poor relief to the city's indigent; the Cleveland Ladies Temperance Union; and the Ladies Aid Society, which provided Union soldiers and their families with food and other supplies during the Civil War. (Western Reserve Historical Society.)

Mrs. Rebecca Elliot Rouse - at. seventy five.

PROTESTANT ORPHAN ASYLUM. Rouse was also a founder of this orphanage, which opened its doors in 1852 to children whose parents could not provide for them. The institution is now Beech Brook, which provides residential and off-site treatment for emotionally disturbed children. (*Picturesque Cleveland.*)

37

SCHOFIELD VAULT. This monument is believed to have been designed by prominent architect Levi T. Scofield (1842–1917). "Schofield" is the alternate spelling and apparently the one he preferred for his family burial place. His buildings and public monuments were often done in this elaborate Romanesque style, reminiscent of the Garfield Monument. (Marian J. Morton.)

SOLDIERS AND SAILORS MONUMENT C. 1900. Scofield's robust sculpture stands in the southeast quadrant of Cleveland's Public Square. The 125-foot monument, dedicated in 1894, honors those who fought in the Civil War. The bronze sculptures depict battle scenes. Rebecca Cromwell Rouse is pictured for her role in the Ladies Aid Society. (*Picturesque Cleveland.*)

HANNA MAUSOLEUM. This grand classical mausoleum is the resting place of Marcus Alonzo Hanna (1837–1904) and his family. Hanna made his fortune in electric street railways and became active in Republican politics, serving as Ohio representative to the U.S. Senate from 1897 until his death in 1904. He is often credited with winning the Republican presidential nomination for his friend, Ohio governor William McKinley, in 1896, and he managed McKinley's successful presidential campaigns in 1896 and 1900. (James W. Garrett IV.)

HANNA STATUE. A seated Hanna looks down from his pedestal on Euclid Avenue, south of the Wade Park Lagoon. The statue's base pays tribute to his civic activism: "This monument erected by friends and fellow citizens commemorates [Hanna's] efforts for peace between capital and labor [a reference to his role in the Civic Federation that mediated disputes between management and unions], his useful citizenship and distinguished public service." (Lake View Cemetery.)

CASE HEADSTONE. An impressive headstone marks the burial place of Leonard Case (1786–1864) and his sons, Leonard Jr. (1820–1880) and William (1818–1862). The senior Case served on the Cleveland village council and in the Ohio legislature from 1824 to 1827. He also founded the Commercial Bank of Lake Erie and the Cleveland-Columbus-Cincinnati Railroad and donated generously to local charities. (James W. Garrett IV.)

CASE SCHOOL, c. 1900. Leonard Case Jr. donated $1 million for the establishment of the technical college that became the Case School of Applied Science (later Case Institute of Technology). The institute opened in 1881 on Rockwell Avenue and moved to University Circle in 1885. Case and his brother William helped found the Cleveland Library Association, later named Case Hall, which collected local history and artifacts. The Western Reserve Historical Society and the Cleveland Museum of Natural History evolved out of this institution. (*Picturesque Cleveland.*)

STONE FAMILY GRAVE SITES. The tall granite column memorializes Amasa Stone (1818–1883) and his family. Stone built railroads and bridges and was a major stockholder in Chisolm's Cleveland Rolling Mills. In 1876 one of Stone's railroad bridges collapsed and 92 people died in the tragedy. To the right of the Stone monument, the sculpture of the helmeted figure of the Archangel Michael, arms folded over a sword, marks the burial site of John M. Hay (1838–1905), husband of Stone's daughter Clara Louise (1849–1914). Hay, also an author and historian, served as Secretary of State under President William McKinley. (James W. Garrett IV.)

ADELBERT COLLEGE, c. 1900. Amasa Stone donated $500,000 to move Western Reserve College from Hudson to University Circle. Adelbert College for men honored the memory of Stone's son Adelbert, who died in a boating accident while a student at Yale University. Saddened by this personal loss as well as by the bridge accident, Amasa Stone took his own life in 1883. (*Picturesque Cleveland.*)

41

MATHER FAMILY MONUMENT. This Celtic cross, marked with an ascending angel symbolizing the triumph of faith over death, marks the burial site of two of Cleveland's most generous philanthropists, Samuel Mather (1851–1931) and his wife Flora (1852–1909), the daughter of Amasa Stone. Samuel was a founder of the Pickands Mather Company, a leading manufacturer of steel, and a benefactor of the University Hospitals, Trinity Cathedral, the Hiram House settlement, and many other institutions. (James W. Garrett IV.)

FLORA STONE MATHER. Flora Stone Mather is pictured here with her sons Samuel Livingston (on the right) and Amasa Stone. Until her death, she engaged in a wide range of civic and philanthropic activities, including the founding of the Goodrich House settlement. (Western Reserve Historical Society.)

COLLEGE FOR WOMEN. Western Reserve University's College for Women was renamed Flora Stone Mather College in 1932 to recognize her interest in and generosity to the institution. From left to right are pictured Clark Hall, Haydn Hall, and Guilford House. Haydn Hall was named for Mather's pastor at First Presbyterian (Old Stone) Church, Hiram C. Haydn, who had barred women from Western Reserve College but had established the College for Women; Guilford Hall was named for Mather's favorite teacher at the Cleveland Academy, Linda Guilford. Mather also gave the college Amasa Stone Chapel to honor her father's memory. After the federation of Western Reserve University and Case Institute of Technology in 1967, Flora Stone Mather College and Adelbert College became part of Case Western Reserve University. (Western Reserve Historical Society.)

ROCKEFELLER OBELISK. This 70-foot obelisk, the Egyptian symbol of power and the tallest structure at Lake View, was created for the Rockefeller family by sculptor Joseph Carabelli. The obelisk is a popular Christian monumental form since it points toward heaven and the afterlife. John D. Rockefeller (1839–1937) came to Cleveland in 1853 and attended high school for two years. He began his business career as a commission merchant, and in 1865 went into the oil business full-time. He amassed great wealth by founding Standard Oil of Ohio, headquartered in Cleveland, gave generously to local cultural and charitable institutions, and donated the land for Rockefeller Park to the city of Cleveland. Allegedly miffed over a property tax bill from Cuyahoga County, however, he gave a very significant donation to the University of Chicago, rather than a local university, and left Cleveland under a cloud. After his death, Rockefeller returned to Lake View and Cleveland for good. Visitors to the cemetery often place dimes at the base of the monument, perhaps hoping that their monies will increase as Rockefeller's did. (Lake View Cemetery.)

STANDARD OIL OF OHIO REFINERIES, 1889. Rockefeller's Standard Oil of Ohio was chartered in 1870. The company quickly bought out much of its local and national competition and in 1882 controlled 90 percent of the nation's oil production. In 1892 the state of Ohio ordered the monopoly dissolved, and in response, Standard Oil of Ohio was reorganized as a holding company, Standard Oil of New Jersey. When this was dissolved by the federal government in 1911 for violating anti-trust legislation, Standard Oil of Ohio (Sohio) became an independent company, its success guaranteed by the growing use of the automobile. The company made the fortunes of many Clevelanders and employed hundreds of workers. Its refineries also polluted the air and the Cuyahoga River. (Western Reserve Historical Society.)

ROCKEFELLER HOME. Rockefeller's summer home in East Cleveland, Forest Hill, was built as a water cure hotel; its porches were designed to catch the healthy breezes from Lake Erie. Although he made his home in New York City in 1884, Rockefeller also maintained this residence until 1917. The Rockefeller family played a key role in developing Cleveland Heights and gave Forest Hill Park to Cleveland Heights and East Cleveland. (Special Collections, Cleveland State University.)

JOHN D. ROCKEFELLER. Rockefeller served on the Lake View board of trustees from 1878 to 1922. This informal picture of Rockefeller and a neighboring property owner, taken in the 1930s, is preserved in the Lake View archives. (Lake View Cemetery.)

VAN SWERINGEN HEADSTONE. This massive stone marks the burial place of real estate entrepreneurs, Oris P. (1879–1936) and Mantis J. (1881–1935) Van Sweringen, the developers of Shaker Heights. The brothers planned the successful community around public transportation and imposed strict regulations on land use and architectural styles. (James W. Garrett IV.)

TERMINAL TOWER. Long Cleveland's signature building, the Terminal Tower complex on Public Square was built by the Van Sweringens as the terminus for their rapid transit system and other railroads. The complex also included the Hotel Cleveland, Higbee's Department Store, and other retail stores and restaurants. Scofield's Soldiers and Sailors Monument is on the left. This complex is now Tower City, owned by Forest City Enterprises. (Western Reserve Historical Society.)

SEVERANCE GRAVE SITE. John L. Severance (1863–1936) and his wife Elizabeth (1865–1929) are buried near this simple, elegant monument. Roses, the symbol of love, enfold the base of the cross. The three steps below the cross and the base of the welcoming bench were carved from a single piece of granite. A Cleveland native, Severance attended Cleveland public schools and graduated from Oberlin College. He worked for Standard Oil of Ohio and then branched off into related industries, founding the Cleveland Linseed Company, a paint and varnish manufacturer. He also served on Lake View's board of trustees. He was particularly interested in the arts and served as president of the Cleveland Museum of Art, to which he donated much of his personal art collection and a half interest in his Cleveland Heights estate, Longwood. (James W. Garrett IV.)

SEVERANCE ESTATE. Severance's Longwood was located on 140 acres at Mayfield and Taylor Roads, about two miles east of Lake View. Designed by distinguished architects Milton Dyer and Charles Schweinfurth, the vast Tudor mansion was completed in 1915 and razed in 1961. The site is now Severance Town Center, which includes a strip mall, apartments, cluster housing, and the Cleveland Heights City Hall. (Special Collections, Cleveland State University.)

SEVERANCE HALL, 1931. To honor the memory of his wife, Severance donated $2.5 million toward the building of Severance Hall, the home of the Cleveland Orchestra. Designed by the architectural firm of Walker and Weeks, the hall is pictured here shortly after its completion. (Western Reserve Historical Society.)

HUGHES MARKER. To heighten the interest of its visitors, Lake View marks the burial sites of some of its notable residents with signs such as this one, which calls attention to the grave site of Adella Prentiss Hughes (1869–1950). The granddaughter of Benjamin and Rebecca Rouse, Hughes was trained as a professional pianist. In 1915, she formed the Musical Arts Association, which was instrumental in the formation of the Cleveland Orchestra three years later. (James W. Garrett IV.)

CLEVELAND ORCHESTRA, 1931. Pictured here on the new, rather austere stage of Severance Hall, the orchestra was conducted by Nikolai Sokoloff (center), whom Hughes had persuaded to come to Cleveland. The Cleveland Orchestra has since won international acclaim for its performances and recordings. (Western Reserve Historical Society.)

SHERWIN FAMILY GRAVE SITE. This rough-hewn stone marks the burial site of the family of Henry A. Sherwin (1842–1916). In 1866 Sherwin founded the Sherwin-Williams Company, which still sells paints around the world. (James W. Garrett IV.)

BELLE SHERWIN (1868–1955). Sherwin's daughter Belle was an activist for women's causes. She was president of the Ohio Consumers' League, a suffragist, a founder of the Women's City Club, and president of the national League of Women Voters, 1924–1934. (Western Reserve Historical Society.)

CRILE MARKER. A sign also marks the grave site of Dr. George W. Crile (1864–1943). Crile was a medical pioneer, performing the first successful blood transfusion in Cleveland's St. Alexis Hospital in 1906. Crile also organized the Lakeside Unit of nurses and doctors who served as volunteers during World War I, for which he received the French Legion of Honor in 1922. (James W. Garrett IV.)

DR. GEORGE W. CRILE. Crile also won many awards for his other published research, including the Cartwright Prize of Columbia University (1897 and 1903). He served as president of the American College of Surgeons (1916–1917), of which he was a founding member. (Western Reserve Historical Society.)

CLEVELAND CLINIC, 1929. Crile was also a co-founder of the Cleveland Clinic Foundation. The clinic was a medical group practice intended to provide specialized medical care within a research and teaching facility. Opened in 1924, the 184-bed hospital is pictured here at Euclid Avenue and East Ninety-fifth Street shortly before a fire on May 15, 1929 killed 123 patients, doctors, and nurses. The tragedy, caused by the exposure of x-ray film to a light bulb, prompted new local and national safety regulations in hospitals. The clinic slowly rebuilt, and since World War II, it has become a huge medical facility with a national and international reputation and clientele. (Western Reserve Historical Society.)

BOLTON FAMILY PLOT. These graceful steps lead to the Bolton family burial plots. Buried here are Chester C. Bolton (1882–1939) and his wife Frances P. (1885–1977). Chester C. Bolton was active in Republican politics. He chaired the National Republican Campaign Committee and brought the Republican National Convention to Cleveland in 1936. He was elected to Congress in 1928, lost his seat in 1936, and then regained it in 1938. (Lake View Cemetery.)

WESTERN RESERVE UNIVERSITY SCHOOL OF NURSING. As the result of her volunteer work with the Visiting Nurse Association, Frances P. Bolton gave both private and public support to the nursing profession. She donated funds to Western Reserve University to establish a school of nursing, pictured here in 1923. In 1935 this facility was named the Frances Payne Bolton School of Nursing in her honor. (Western Reserve Historical Society.)

FRANCES PAYNE BOLTON. When her husband died in 1939, Frances Payne Bolton took his Congressional seat and then became the first woman from Ohio to be elected to Congress, retaining the seat until 1968. A long-time member of the House Foreign Affairs Committee, Bolton traveled to Europe, the Soviet Union, the Near East, and Africa. In 1953, she became the first congresswoman appointed to the United Nations General Assembly. An enthusiastic supporter of civil rights, she was awarded the Certificate of Honor of the National Association of Colored Graduate Nurses (1951) and an honorary LHD from Tuskegee Institute (1957). Bolton is pictured here observing a nuclear test in Nevada in May 1953. (Western Reserve Historical Society.)

JELLIFFE MONUMENT AND HEADSTONES. Russell Jelliffe (1891–1980) and his wife Rowena (1892–1992) are buried here. Arriving in Cleveland in 1915 with master's degrees in social work from the University of Chicago, the Jelliffes opened the Playhouse Settlement in Cleveland's Central neighborhood. The Jelliffes discovered that the arts, especially theater, brought whites and African Americans together, and the settlement, renamed Karamu House in 1941, became an interracial theater that produced the works of Zora Neale Hurston and Langston Hughes, among others. (James W. Garrett IV.)

KARAMU HOUSE. Rowena (third from the left) and Russell Jelliffe (on the far right) are pictured here at the groundbreaking for an arts center at Karamu. When the Jelliffes retired in 1963, Karamu had become an internationally known theater and center for African-American culture. (Western Reserve Historical Society.)

CRAWFORD BURIAL PLACE. A marble bench marks the burial place of Frederick C. Crawford (1891–1994). In 1933 Crawford became president of Thompson Products, a manufacturer of automotive and aviation parts. In 1953 a merger produced Thompson–Ramo–Wooldridge, or TRW Inc. (James. W. Garrett IV.)

FREDERICK C. CRAWFORD. One of Crawford's passions was collecting antique cars and airplanes, which he donated to the Western Reserve Historical Society. They are now housed in its Frederick C. Crawford Auto Aviation Museum. (Western Reserve Historical Society.)

STOKES HEADSTONE. The headstone of Carl B. Stokes (1927–1996) describes him as Ambassador, because at the time of his death in 1996 he served as ambassador to the Seychelles Islands. Stokes was better known as mayor of Cleveland, serving from 1967 to 1971, the first African American to be elected mayor of a large city. The inscription reads: "He fought, never gave up, may not have won, but fought a good fight." (Joseph E. Barmann.)

CARL B. STOKES. Elected in the wake of the Hough riots of 1966, Stokes initially brought racial peace to the city, but a second riot in 1968 cost Stokes political support in the white community. Stokes encouraged blacks in Cleveland and elsewhere to follow in his political footsteps. (Western Reserve Historical Society.)

Three

CHANGING RESIDENTS

SLEEPING CHILD. This tiny sculpture depicts Francis Bentley Craw (1839–1847), apparently re-interred from another cemetery. Today, the children and adults buried at Lake View reflect the changing racial and ethnic composition of Cleveland. (Lake View Cemetery.)

1911 FUNERAL. As this stately procession indicates, automobiles initially made Lake View more accessible to city-dwellers, significantly broadening the cemetery's potential clientele. The automobile also spurred the rapid growth of Lake View's neighbors, East Cleveland and Cleveland Heights, especially during the 1920s. As the population of these suburbs and the city of Cleveland changed to include middle- and working-class, white and non-white residents, Lake View's population changed as well. In the years after World War II, however, federally funded freeways encouraged urban and suburban residents to move farther and farther east and south, away from the city, the older suburbs, and Lake View. (Lake View Cemetery.)

LAKE VIEW, 1938. This landscape shows off the variety of grand monuments—obelisks, statues, funerary urns, and classically inspired headstones—built during the cemetery's first decades. The Gordon monument to the left memorializes William J. Gordon (1818–1892), a member of Lake View's board of trustees and the donor of Gordon Park to the city of Cleveland. (Lake View Cemetery.)

LAKE VIEW, 1941. In contrast, Lake View also had sections that catered to a more modest clientele. Smooth lawns and simpler ground-level headstones resemble a more contemporary lawn park cemetery, ornamentation provided by the trees and hedges. (Lake View Cemetery.)

BURIAL OF UNIDENTIFIED
COLLINWOOD FIRE.

COLLINWOOD SCHOOL FIRE. This postcard memorialized the burial of the victims of a fire in the village of Collinwood which occurred March 4, 1908—ironically, Ash Wednesday. Dignitaries stand before a huge cross and arches of flowers and in front of the small caskets. The origin of this fire, in a relatively new building, is still unknown, and the children had practiced fire drills. Heroic teachers managed to get half of their students out of the building safely, but other terrified children, in an effort to escape, fell down the stairs and piled up, one upon the other. As distraught parents and neighbors looked on and the equipment of the volunteer fire department failed, 172 children and three adults perished. Many of the victims were burned beyond recognition. Twenty-three were buried at Lake View in this mass grave in a plot purchased by the village of Collinwood. This tragedy turned the nation's attention to school safety. In 1910 Collinwood was annexed by the city of Cleveland, which had a professional fire-fighting force. (Special Collections, Cleveland State University.)

COLLINWOOD SCHOOL MEMORIAL. This more dignified monument was created later "in memory of those teachers and children who lost their lives in the Collinwood fire." The sculpture depicts a welcoming angel, arms encircling the children. The names of the victims are listed on the back of the memorial. (Marian J. Morton.)

"OUR DOLLY." This child also died in the Collinwood fire, but she is memorialized alone. The inscription on this small marble figure, already wearing angel's wings, is almost illegible, but she always carries this bouquet of artificial flowers. (James W. Garrett IV.)

POLIMENE HEADSTONE. In 1949, Lake View trustees designated a special section of the cemetery for children. Here parents have left poignant memorials to children taken from them too soon, such as this one. (James W. Garrett IV.)

HUGHES HEADSTONE. Although their lives were short, children come alive in these small, touching headstones, mourned but remembered by their parents. (James W. Garrett IV.)

VIEW OF LITTLE ITALY, 1917. This view looks southwest, over an almost undeveloped section of the cemetery, toward Alta House on Mayfield Road in Little Italy. On the left are the trees of the "heights" of Cleveland Heights. The wall that now faces on Mayfield Road had not yet been built. The goal of Alta House, named after John D. Rockefeller's daughter Alta because he was a donor to the settlement, was to ease the transition of Italians into American life. In 1920, Cleveland was home to more than 18,000 persons who had been born in Italy. The largest Italian settlement was Big Italy, located along Woodland and Orange Avenues, near the city's produce markets, where many Italians found work. Little Italy, located from East 119th to East 125th Streets on Mayfield and Murray Hill Roads, grew up next door to the cemetery and became home to its stonecutters and gardeners. (Lake View Cemetery.)

LAKE VIEW AND LITTLE ITALY. Although Lake View provided jobs for some residents of Little Italy, relationships between the cemetery and its Italian neighbors have sometimes been uneasy. This wall now separates them. Inside the wall and close to Little Italy, however, is this predominantly Italian section of the cemetery, and many Italians are buried elsewhere throughout the cemetery. (James W. Garrett IV.)

CASINO HEADSTONE. Located in the Italian section of Lake View is this headstone, which remembers this husband and wife who died together in the 1929 Cleveland Clinic fire. (James W. Garrett IV.)

CARABELLI BURIAL SITE. This simple headstone of Stoney Creek granite marks the burial place of Joseph Carabelli (1850–1911), the "father of Little Italy." The use of the bronze lettering and ornament on granite was unique for its time. Carabelli was trained in Italy as a stone mason and sculptor, and in 1880 established his monument firm across Euclid Avenue from the cemetery. Carabelli employed other stonecutters who also settled near Lake View. Carabelli was instrumental in the establishment of Alta House and Holy Rosary Church (although he was not Catholic). He was elected to the Ohio House of Representatives in 1908. (James W. Garrett IV.)

MONUMENT BY CARABELLI. The Lake View board of trustees approved this monument for Rufus K. Winslow in 1899. The dramatic granite cross is ornamented only with a bronze branch. The stark fall landscape shows off the dazzling variety of Lake View's monuments. (Lake View Cemetery.)

BRUSH MONUMENT. Carabelli and his company (now Johns-Carabelli Company Mayfair Memorials) built many of Lake View's most stunning monuments. Carabelli's work includes the Jeptha Wade monument, the Wade Chapel, and the Rockefeller obelisk. Pictured here is Carabelli's classically-inspired monument for Charles Frances Brush (1849–1929), inventor of the arc light. Brush demonstrated the practicality of his arc light at Cleveland's Public Square in 1879, and it was soon in use throughout the country. His company, Brush Electric, was ultimately merged into General Electric. In this photograph, Brush's towering monument, standing at the edge of a deep ravine, is illuminated by the setting sun. (Lake View Cemetery.)

DELMASTRO MONUMENT. Believing in close connections between the living and the dead, Italians often commemorate their loved ones with striking photo-engraved portraits such as this one of a former member of the United States Air Force. The sculptor of this contemporary headstone creates drama by using contrasting colors of jet black and Vermont gray granite as well as the new technology of photo-engraving. The curve of the black granite mimics the thrust of the pilot in flight. (James W. Garret IV.)

SCHWALM HEADSTONE. Germans began to arrive in Cleveland in considerable numbers in the 1830s and became one of the city's largest immigrant groups. The use of German on this 1915 headstone signals the family's desire to retain their native culture. (James W. Garrett IV.)

TIEFENTHALER HEADSTONE. Because many German immigrants were skilled artisans or property owners, they were readily assimilated into American life, except during the anti-German hysteria of World War I. The family of this woman who died in 1913, however, preferred to remember "Mutter" in German. (James W. Garrett IV.)

VAGIANOS HEADSTONE. The immigration of Greeks to Cleveland dates from the late nineteenth century. This contemporary headstone with Greek inscriptions also indicates pride in the native tongue and culture. (James W. Garrett IV.)

CHANG HEADSTONE. Cleveland's most recent immigrants have come from Asia. Like earlier arrivals, they often wish to be remembered in death in their native language, as this Chinese couple has. Lake View's headstones chart the waves of immigration to Cleveland and the United States. (James W. Garret IV.)

LATVIAN MONUMENT. Small numbers of Latvian immigrants arrived in Cleveland in the late nineteenth and early twentieth centuries and found jobs in local industries such as steel mills. Latvia was invaded and taken over by the Soviet Union in 1940, and after World War II, local Latvians organized to bring an estimated 2,500 newcomers to Cleveland. Organized institutions such as the Latvian Evangelical Lutheran Church, and, in 1951, the Latvian Baptist Church, built this monument. It bears the Christian message of salvation in their native language, as well as the names of many church members who are buried in Lake View. Latvians also sponsor many social, political, and cultural organizations that cherish the memory of their homeland. (James W. Garret IV.)

SUBURBAN TEMPLE-KOL AMI SECTION.
In 1960, Lake View trustees set aside
this section for the congregation at its
own request. Just to the east of Lake
View, a Reform Jewish congregation had
established Mayfield Cemetery in 1887,
a harbinger of the middle-class Jewish
emigration from the city to the suburbs.
In 1920 Jews constituted an estimated
10 percent of Cleveland's population. In
the next four decades, many Jews and
Jewish institutions moved into Cleveland
Heights. (James W. Garrett IV.)

GROTTE HEADSTONE. The Star of David and the use of Hebrew deliberately call attention to
the deceased's religious and ethnic identity in a section that is predominantly Jewish, within in
a cemetery that is predominantly Christian. (James W. Garret IV.)

73

GOLDSTEIN SCULPTURE. In addition to simple headstones, the Suburban Temple-Kol Ami section contains dramatic monuments such as this. The three bronze birds, created by artist William McVey, represent the family's three sons, in flight. The tops corners of the stone curve inward toward each other, symbolizing the closeness of the husband and wife, Saul S. Goldstein (1912–1988) and Dorothy Pyner Goldstein (1914–1994). (James W. Garret IV.)

MANN SCULPTURE. This contemporary, irregularly shaped stone that marks the burial place of Samuel Mann (1911–1987) was designed to catch and reflect light. On its polished granite surfaces are reflected Lake View's trees and lawns, as well as the photographer (on the left). (James W. Garret IV.)

SECTION 50. There are African Americans buried throughout Lake View. However, in 1960, the cemetery trustees reserved the new Section 50 "for negroes." This decision responded to the changing racial composition of Cleveland and surrounding communities: in 1970, almost 40 percent of Cleveland's population was African American, and African Americans were moving into East Cleveland and Cleveland Heights. (James W. Garret IV.)

MORGAN HEADSTONE. Garrett A. Morgan (1877–1963) and his wife Mary A. (1884–1968) are buried in Section 50. His headstone reads: "By his deeds he shall be remembered." His deeds were many. (James W. Garrett IV.)

GARRETT A. MORGAN. Entrepreneur and political activist, Morgan invented the traffic light and a "Breathing Device," or gas mask, among other things. Wearing the mask, he rescued several workers trapped in a gas-filled tunnel under Lake Erie in 1916, for which he received only belated public recognition. The mask was also used during World War I. Morgan sold the rights to the traffic light to General Electric in 1923. Morgan supported many black organizations, including the Cleveland NAACP. In 1920, he founded the *Cleveland Call*, a forerunner of the *Cleveland Call and Post*. In 1931, he ran unsuccessfully for Cleveland City Council. The Garrett Morgan Cleveland School of Science is named after him. (Lake View Cemetery.)

CHESNUTT MARKER. This sign marks the burial site of Charles Chesnutt (1858–1932). (His name is misspelled on the sign.) Chesnutt was born in Cleveland and after finishing his education and teaching briefly elsewhere, he returned to the city in 1883. Admitted to the Ohio bar in 1887, he was a successful lawyer and court stenographer. This section of Lake View is racially integrated, as was Chesnutt's neighborhood in Cleveland. Chesnutt sent his two daughters, Helen and Dorothy, to Smith College and his son Edwin to Harvard University. They are buried nearby as is Chesnutt's wife, Susan (1861–1941). (James W. Garrett IV.)

CHARLES W. CHESNUTT. Probably the best-known African American in Cleveland during his lifetime, Chesnutt gained national fame as a writer of short stories and novels that focused on racial themes. He also served on the board of the Cleveland NAACP and was active in several other inter-racial organizations. (Western Reserve Historical Society.)

FLEMING HEADSTONE. Lethia C. Fleming (1876–1963) was the wife of Thomas W. Fleming (1874-1948), the first African American elected to Cleveland City Council. She was a political leader in her own right. A member of the National Association of Colored Women, she was also an early suffragist. (James W. Garrett IV.)

LETHIA C. FLEMING. Fleming was an ardent Republican and organized the National Association of Republican Women in the United States. A social worker with the Cuyahoga County Child Welfare Board by profession, Fleming also helped found the local Negro Welfare Association, which later affiliated with the national Urban League. (Western Reserve Historical Society.)

WALKER HEADSTON. Hazel Mountain Walker (1889–1980), also an activist for the Republican Party, is buried near Lethia Fleming. Walker earned a law degree and passed the bar exam in 1919, but was an educator by profession, having earned bachelor's and master's degrees in education from Western Reserve University. In 1936, she became the principal of Rutherford B. Hayes elementary school, the first African American to receive such an appointment. (James W. Garrett IV.)

HAZEL MOUNTAIN WALKER. Walker also had a career as an actress, appearing often in Karamu House productions. She is credited with giving the institution its name, which means "a place of joyful meeting" in Swahili. (Lake View Cemetery.)

WILLIAM O. WALKER FUNERAL. William Otis Walker (1896–1981) is buried in Section 50. His graveside service was attended by a large crowd of blacks and whites, as seen here. Walker was the long-time editor of the *Cleveland Call and Post*, a founder of the Future Outlook League, and a Republican member of Cleveland City Council from 1940–1947. As director of industrial relations from 1963–1971, Walker became the first African American to hold a cabinet-level position in the state government. A political conservative, Walker nevertheless supported black causes such as the NAACP and the Urban League and sometimes black Democrats such as Carl Stokes. Walker was elected to the Gallery of Distinguished Newspaper Publishers at Howard University. (Special Collections, Cleveland State University.)

MEMORIAL DAY, 1935. This holiday when Americans honor those who served in the armed forces has always had special meaning at Lake View. On this Memorial Day, women from the American Legion Auxiliary placed a wreath at the grave of an Unknown Soldier in front of the Garfield Monument at Lake View. (The grave is no longer there.) The veterans buried at Lake View came from all walks of life. (Special Collections, Cleveland State University.)

CIVIL WAR CASUALTY. This handsome family monument, created in 1883, remembers son Charles P. Bowler, "killed in battle at Cedar Mountain, Aug. 9, 1862, aged 29 years." (Marian J. Morton.)

WORLD WAR II VETERAN. Veterans of all the major twentieth-century wars are buried here. This headstone memorializes Alice A. McKinney, one of the 350,000 American women who served in World War II. (James W. Garrett IV.)

GULF WAR II. Brandon Ulysses Sloan, age 19, died in the first war of the twenty-first century: Gulf War II. The headstone, marked with a United States flag, is personalized by photographs of Sloan and the things he loved, and the tribute, "our hero." (James W. Garrett IV.)

Four

CHANGING
LANDSCAPES

LAKE VIEW LANDSCAPE, 1874. In 1872, Lake View trustees borrowed landscape gardener Adolph Strauch from Cincinnati's Spring Grove Cemetery, to create the first design for the cemetery. The "double vision" of this stereopticon shows how water was used to dramatize the monuments. This view may be looking northwest from Wade Lake. Lake View's landscape changed dramatically over the next century and a quarter. (Western Reserve Historical Society.)

LAKE VIEW LANDSCAPE, c. 1900. Only the Garfield Monument appears over the woods and lake at the turn of the twentieth century when the cemetery remained relatively undeveloped. Strauch insisted that all monuments be approved by the cemetery trustees, that plots be uniform in size, and that family plots not be enclosed by fences as was customary in older cemeteries. (Western Reserve Historical Society.)

SUBURBAN LANDSCAPE. Cemetery design influenced suburban landscaping, as is evident in this Cleveland Heights home, c. 1911, with its carefully designed rural setting, complete with ponds and dramatic stairways. (Case Western Reserve University Special Collections.)

WEEPING HEMLOCK. This tree is over 100 years old and may be one of the largest specimens of its kind in the United States. Strauch and subsequent gardeners introduced hundreds of varieties of shrubs, plants, and trees, like these, to Lake View. Most are carefully labeled for visitors, and the cemetery sponsors many horticultural tours. (Lake View Cemetery.)

PEEGEE HYDRANGEA. The use of indigenous and exotic trees, including the Japanese pagoda, a Chinese maackia, a Kentucky coffee tree, the Lake View ginko, and a purple-leaf European beech, carry forward the founders' original plan to enhance the natural landscape. (Lake View Cemetery.)

TREES IN BLOOM. In late spring, dogwood, carmine crab apples, and magnolias bloom. Here they grace the entrance to the Wade Chapel. Compare this photograph with the one taken shortly after Wade Chapel was completed and before the plantings. In 1903, Lake View hired a German nurseryman, Ernst Muny, under whose direction the cemetery bought thousands of trees, shrubs, and flowers; 6,000 were planted in 1910 alone. Careful planning has ensured that there are trees and shrubs blooming much of the year. These introduce a variety of colors, shapes, and textures into the predominantly green landscape. (Laura Roberts Dempsey.)

FLOWERING PLANTS. Family plots often contain shrubs and flowers, like these snowball hydrangeas. Families make financial arrangements to ensure that Lake View is responsible for the maintenance of their plots. This landscape also shows the way that Lake View's trees of varying shapes and heights complement the variety of headstones and monuments. (Lake View Cemetery.)

DAFFODIL HILL. Every April, Lake View's tens of thousands of daffodils, representing 50 varieties, are on display, seen here on Daffodil Hill. The collection was initiated by gifts from Dr. William H. Weir, after whom a roadway in the cemetery is named. (Laura Roberts Dempsey.)

GARDENER AND DAFFODILS. Lake View employs a large crew of gardeners and grounds-keepers. Pictured here among the daffodils are Domenic Ramachati, who worked as a nurseryman and groundskeeper at the cemetery for 70 years, and a young friend. Lake View maintains a memorial garden to Ramachati near Little Italy. (Lake View Cemetery.)

GARDENERS AT WORK. Like all gardeners, the cemetery staff must combat rain, snow, heat, drought, and insects. Tree planting and other landscaping can be done only when the Cleveland weather permits. (Lake View Cemetery.)

MAYFIELD FENCE, 1961. The cemetery infrastructure requires constant maintenance: roadways, outbuildings, equipment, gates, and the wall and iron fence along Mayfield Road pictured here. (Lake View Cemetery.)

WILDLIFE. Canada geese live at the cemetery's two lakes. Many geese no longer bother to fly south during the winter. This park in an urban setting is also home to innumerable squirrels, rabbits, and chipmunks, as well as many varieties of birds and an occasional deer. (Lake View Cemetery.)

DUGWAY BROOK. Dugway Brook ran through the old stone quarry in the cemetery, carrying water from the suburbs to the east. In heavy rainstorms, the brook often flooded, causing serious damage and inconvenience, to Lake View and University Circle to the west. (Lake View Cemetery.)

LAKE VIEW DAM. In 1975, the cemetery trustees sued Cleveland Heights and University Heights to halt the expansion of their sewer system, based on the grounds that the expansion would exacerbate the flooding of Dugway Brook. A court order created the Cleveland Regional Sewer District to build this dam to solve the problem. Lake View donated ten acres of its property to the project. When the dam opened in 1978, critics thought it was too big—80 feet high, taller than many downtown office buildings, and 500 feet across. Critics also thought the dam too expensive; its initial cost was $6.3 million. Although seldom used to its capacity, the dam's 67,000 cubic yards of poured concrete dramatically altered the existing landscape. Yet, like Lake View's mausoleums, obelisks, and statuary, the dam remains a monument to human ingenuity and the desire for immortality. (Lake View Cemetery.)

ROMANESQUE MONUMENT. Styles in monuments have changed dramatically over the last century and a half. This Victorian Romanesque structure, its solemnity enhanced by the bleak fall landscape, was popular from the time of Lake View's founding through the 1890s. Garfield's temporary and permanent burial places were also created in this style, as was the Schofield vault. The massive use of stone suggests permanence; the use of ornamentation, affluence; and the spire pointing toward heaven, the Christian belief in the afterlife. This monument is reminiscent of Cleveland churches built during the same time period, such as the Cathedral of St. John the Evangelist, Trinity Episcopal Cathedral, and First Presbyterian (Old Stone) Church. (Lake View Cemetery.)

CLASSICAL MAUSOLEUM. A mausoleum, like the Wade Chapel, became the choice of many families in the early twentieth century. Enthusiasm for classical art and sculpture was encouraged by the 1893 Columbian Exposition in Chicago, where exhibits were housed in huge, temporary classical structures. Cleveland's public buildings like the City Hall, the Public Library, and the Board of Education were also done in classical revival styles. (Lake View Cemetery.)

CLASSICAL GARDEN. Private gardens, like those at John L. Severance's Cleveland Heights estate Longwood, also emulated neoclassicism in design and statuary. (Case Western Reserve University Special Collections.)

CLASSICAL FIGURE. Many of Lake View's sculptures also express the contemporary passion for the classical age. This style allowed the artist to create an attractive human form but to cover it modestly in Greek or Roman garb, such as that worn by the thoughtful figure here on the Topliff monument. Carrying a cross, signifying her faith in the afterlife, she looks hopefully toward heaven. This representation, inspired by the distant past, also distanced death itself. (James W. Garrett IV.)

94

MOTHER AND CHILD. Like the garden cemetery itself, these sculptures were created to soften the tragedy of death by beautifying and sentimentalizing it. This moving figure of a mother embracing her child provides comfort to the grieving. This sculpture is a memorial to the family of Joseph Card; two angels on the stone pedestal may represent John E. Card, aged nine, "Our treasure," and Harry H. Card, aged 12, "Our other treasure," whose small headstones are nearby. (Lake View Cemetery.)

FAITH AND HOPE. Most cemetery sculptures did not represent the specific persons whom they memorialized, but abstract virtues intended to inspire or console the deceased's family or other viewers. These female figures, Bibles in hand, symbolize faith and hope. The sculptor has created a dramatic contrast by depicting one figure looking down in sorrow and the other looking hopefully toward heaven. Like all monuments to the dead, however, this choice of symbols reveals something of the life of the Morris family who are buried here—in this instance, a belief in the Christian afterlife promised in the New Testament. (Lake View Cemetery.)

SORROWING WOMEN. Joseph Carabelli created this dramatic memorial by placing these life-like figures not high on a pedestal, but on the ground at eye-level. They stand close together, in front of the massive rectangular sarcophagus of the E.M. Peck family. One woman carries the funerary urn, the other's face is cloaked and indistinguishable as she kneels over a tablet that reads: "Peace my soul be still." The monument bears the olive wreaths that symbolize the triumph of life over death. Yet the figures create the impression of unrelieved grief, perhaps explained by the headstones in front of them. These headstones record the births and deaths of E.M. Peck and his wife Susan, and their two children, who sadly predeceased them: their four-year-old daughter and their 17-year-old son. Their verisimilitude and their shared grief make these perhaps the most arresting of Lake View's Victorian figures. These figures also provide stunning evidence of Carabelli's skill as a sculptor. (James W. Garrett IV.)

MAIDEN WITH A LILY. This striking figure, created in a style that pre-dates Christianity, is nevertheless a Christian symbol. She stands modestly, carved into the surface of an immense, irregularly shaped stone that represents Christ's sepulcher. This unusual monument marks the burial place of the family of industrialist Moses C. Younglove (1811–1892), who also served on Lake View's first board of trustees. (Roy Woda.)

ST. JOHN THE EVANGELIST. This vibrant sculpture represents the saint with his pen, scroll, and eagle. He looks not sorrowful but strong and brave; perhaps the favorite saint of the Castle family buried here. Like the cemetery itself, these Victorian sculptures were meant to inspire virtue in those who saw them. (Lake View Cemetery.)

SILAS S. STONE SCULPTURE. This robust portrait of real estate dealer Stone (1815–1884) is an unusual example of a sculpture that represents an individual, rather than an abstraction from the distant past. The Garfield and the Chisolm statues are also in this genre. The figure exhibits the fine craftsmanship of the sculptor as well as Stone's own sturdy ego. Stone is clearly master of all he surveys, in death as presumably in life. The message is secular, not religious, which makes the monument even more extraordinary for its era. (Lake View Cemetery.)

HERALDING ANGEL. Most cemetery figures were female, women being thought more virtuous than men in this period. This handsome figure, however, is decidedly male, his masculinity accentuated by his height—about 30 feet—and by the large trumpet he carries to call his listeners home to heaven. This is the burial place of the James F. Clark family. (Lake View Cemetery.)

PERKINS STATUE. In contrast to the overpowering angel, this slight, graceful bronze figure, cast in Rome in 1901, bears a secular message. The classical figure on the family plot of Jacob B. Perkins (1854–1936) represents the American spirit of liberty and holds aloft the torch of freedom. (James W. Garrett IV.)

CELEBRATING LIFE. Contemporary monuments, like contemporary eschatology, are more likely to celebrate life than mourn death. An example is this charming sculpture of a child feeding a squirrel, which was originally a garden piece. This sculpture now enlivens this grave site of the Tuckerman family and is in striking contrast to the solemn Victorian sculptures. (Lake View Cemetery.)

EVANS SCULPTURE. Monuments today, like this one of the family of William Howard Evans (1911–1996), also tend to be less abstract and more personal. The nude bronze figures on this whimsical, very unique monument were taken from a wall by the family's swimming pool. The children have turned their backs on life and look hopefully into the future: "Over the wall, the intrigue of the unknown" compels their attention. (James W. Garret IV.)

ADAMSONS MONUMENT.
This interesting, irregularly
shaped stone makes a
personal statement about this
family's pride in their shared
profession. The monument
proudly announces that father,
mother, and daughter were
doctors, and it also bears the
caduceus, the symbol of the
medical profession. (James W.
Garrett IV.)

PAX MEMORIAL. This handsome
rectangular stone also has a very specific,
personal meaning. The stained glass
inset, created by the deceased, Mary
Peepas Pax (1929–2001), represents her
passion for growing bonsai trees and
keeps her memory alive. To the right is
the Christian symbol of the cross with
inter-twined wedding rings, representing
her marriage. (James W. Garrett IV.)

DELLA SCULPTURE. Here is a contemporary version of a traditional religious icon: a bronze sculpture of the sorrowing mother of Christ holding in her arms her fallen son. The inscription, "Greater love hath no man than this," were the words of Jesus to his disciples on the night before he was crucified. They refer to the Christian belief that Christ sacrificed his life to save his followers, and also to the sacrifices that family members make for one another. The flanking urns are inscribed with olive wreaths that symbolize victory over death; the urns contain plantings and, as has recently become customary, American flags. In front of this dramatic pieta are the headstones of those who are buried here: "Beloved father," Samuel A. Della (1893–1971), and "Precious Mother," Mary L. Della (1913–2000). There is also a headstone for their son, Philip S. Della, who commissioned the sculpture. Although the figures are Renaissance-inspired, the grief expressed is reminiscent of some of the Victorian statuary. (James W. Garrett IV.)

ZELLMAN HEADSTONE. Photo-engraving techniques, imported by artisans from eastern Europe, can reproduce the deceased's picture on the gravestone, as seen here. This monument is enlivened and personalized by the question asked in death, as presumably in life, by the smiling friend, mother, and grandmother: "Did you call?" (James W. Garrett IV.)

WRIGHT HEADSTONE. These photo-engravings recall this couple with loving detail and unpretentious accuracy. "Too well loved to be forgotten. Rest in peace," wish their children and grandchildren. (James W. Garrett IV.)

BLAKEMORE HEADSTONE. Less formal, but equally personal, is this photograph of a young man with a child. The description is brief: "beloved son, father, brother, uncle & friends," but the touching photograph speaks volumes. (James W. Garrett IV.)

HARRIS MEMORIAL. Most twentieth-century headstones simply record the name of the deceased, his or her relationship to others in the plot, and birth and death dates. Recently, the custom of re-telling a life story on the headstone has been revived. Here is an admiring tribute to a teacher, associated for 43 years with the Cleveland public schools: "Master teacher and friend of youth, a man of noblest character dearly beloved. His works do follow him." (James W. Garrett IV.)

REMEMBERING FRIENDSHIP. A group of close friends commissioned this monument for themselves after two of their comrades, still young men, had died. The photo-engraved angel overlooks their memorial to friendship: "Warm sun, shine kindly here / Whispering winds, blow softly here / Gentle rains, fall peaceful here. / Winter snow, glisten brightly here. / Towering trees, grow lofty here. / Fragrant flowers, grow abundantly here. / Birds of the air, sing sweetly here. / And storm clouds, pass quickly here. / For here in the care of this guardian angel, the best of friends lie sleeping. / Their hopes and dreams are buried here but their love and memory we're keeping. Good night, dear friends, good night." Although the design is contemporary, the monument, like the cemetery itself and like older monuments, intends to console and uplift. (James W. Garrett IV.)

GHERLEIN HEADSTONE. This young man died before his 13th birthday. His love of baseball is captured here, as is his long struggle with illness, in the words he wrote himself: "Courage and I have met many times. He is hard to deal with, but it's worth it when you're done." (James W. Garrett IV.)

BENNER-CARTER HEADSTONES. These young men, high school friends, died together in a tragic automobile accident. The crossed hockey sticks represent the Cleveland Heights High School team that they played on. (James W. Garrett IV.)

COMMUNITY MAUSOLEUM. In 1990, Lake View opened this community mausoleum. Located near the Mayfield gate where its modernism did not jar with more traditional monuments, the new structure has granite walls and a glass and steel roof, punctuated by skylights. Shaped like a cruciform, it includes private and family burial rooms and a large non-denominational chapel under a glass dome. The mausoleum responded to the growing preference for cremation and above-ground burial and was also a more efficient use of space than the traditional outdoor plots or mausoleums. (Lake View Cemetery.)

LANDSCAPE, 2003. Since 1869, people have altered Lake View's natural landscape in innumerable ways. They have dug lakes, designed pathways, built gates and fences, planted thousands of flowers and trees, created classical mausoleums, Victorian statuary, towering obelisks, headstones of all kinds and in all languages, and constructed a huge dam. But even in this photograph, with the buildings of downtown Cleveland barely visible in the distance, the natural drama of that ridge high above Lake Erie dominates the scene, exactly as the cemetery's founders had hoped. (James W. Garrett IV.)

Five

A PLACE FOR THE LIVING

LIVE AT LAKE VIEW. The cemetery is full of life. Tens of thousands of people come here every year: to visit grave sites, admire the landscapes and monuments, to picnic, take photographs, walk the dog, sunbathe, or court. Many take tours that the cemetery sponsors, such as this 1988 Mother's Day tour that focused on notable women buried at Lake View. (Lake View Cemetery.)

TROLLEY TOUR. Lake View's monuments and signs recount much of the region's past, of special interest to history buffs such as these members of the Moreland Hills Historical Society. Other tours focus on the trees, plants, and wildlife at Lake View. (Lake View Cemetery.)

MEMORIAL DAYS. On Memorial Day, Lake View and the community still pay special tribute to the men and women of the armed services. These tributes re-affirm the cemetery's patriotism and its link with the nation's past. These Western Reserve Sons of the American Revolution remembered the War for Independence. (Lake View Cemetery.)

RELIVING THE PAST. The Civil War enjoys a special place in American hearts since it pitted the North against the South, brother against brother, and consequently occasioned the greatest loss of life of any American war. Six hundred twenty thousand men died in this war and more than 375,00 were wounded. Ten thousand men from Cuyahoga County, where Cleveland is located, served in the Union army: 1,700 died and 2,000 were wounded. Wives were left widows, and children were left fatherless. Fought almost a century and a half ago, however, the Civil War today seems distant and romantic. Standing in front of the Garfield Monument on Memorial Day in 1987, these men, appropriately costumed and armed as Garfield himself had been, contributed to the romanticization of that war. (Lake View Cemetery.)

LOOKING TO THE FUTURE. These young men of the Junior ROTC Color Guard prepared to enter the armed services and serve in future wars by marching in a Memorial Day parade at Lake View. (Lake View Cemetery.)

MEMORIAL DAY MUSIC. Bagpipers provide music and color for Lake View's Memorial Day festivities. Although the Lake View landscape is always serene, the sounds of the city—church bells, trains, rapid transits, automobiles, and the sirens of emergency vehicles—often fill the air. (Lake View Cemetery.)

HERITAGE DAYS. These community events, like the tours and the historical markers, celebrate the historical significance of those buried in the cemetery. Some are represented by historical interpreters. Pictured here, left to right, by the horse and buggy are the interpreters of Jeptha H. Wade, James Abram Garfield, and John D. Rockefeller. They make the history of the cemetery and the community come alive for visitors. (Lake View Cemetery.)

RE-CREATING THE PAST. On Heritage Day, hot dogs cost a quarter. Cemetery president and CEO William L. Garrison was the chef in 2002. (Lake View Cemetery.)

MUSIC AT LAKE VIEW. This gospel choir sang on Heritage Day on the steps of the Garfield Monument. Their music resonated with the growing African-American presence in the cemetery. (Lake View Cemetery.)

SINGING ANGELS. On July 9, 1994, the monument also provided the setting for a performance by Cleveland's Singing Angels. This choir, composed of children from all over northern Ohio, has performed on television and around the world. (Lake View Cemetery.)

CHILDREN'S CHOIR. The Cory United Methodist Church children's choir presented a Christmas program in the Wade Chapel in front of the Tiffany window that represents the Christian hope of resurrection after death. (Lake View Cemetery.)

MOVING VIETNAM WALL. In July 1996, Lake View hosted the Moving Vietnam Wall with ceremonies attended by scores of elected officials and the general public. This trumpeter played taps as the flag was lowered over the wall. Thousands visited the Moving Wall, many of whom had not seen the original sculpture in Washington D.C. by Maya Lin. Originally controversial, this sculpture is now much admired. Unlike the Civil War, the Vietnam War remains painfully fresh in American memory. (Lake View Cemetery.)

TRIBUTE TO THE DEAD. Honor guards paid tribute to the 58,000 American lives lost during the Vietnam conflict. Their names are inscribed on the wall in chronological rather than alphabetical order because the artist wanted to create a sense of the passage of time. (Lake View Cemetery.)

REMEMBERING LIFE. As at the Vietnam Wall in Washington D.C., family members left mementoes for those whose names appear on the traveling wall. Here is a poignant letter from a mother to her son that is reminiscent of the inscriptions chosen by parents for the headstones of their young children. (Lake View Cemetery.)

117

CELEBRATING THE SPIRIT. From July 2001 through June 2002, Lake View became the site of an outdoor art exhibit, "Celebration of the Spirit." The sometimes startling juxtaposition of very contemporary art work with historic monuments is illustrated here by *Immigrant Gate II, 1997,* by Jim Galluci. Galluci designed the painted steel sculpture to symbolize his art's accessibility. The sculpture was appropriately placed by the Euclid Avenue gate, which has also become increasingly accessible to Cleveland's immigrants from around the world. Co-sponsored by several local foundations and the Ohio Arts Council, the exhibit featured the work of 30 artists from all over the United States. (Lake View Cemetery.)

SIGNS AT THE GATES. The innovative exhibit earned the cemetery both praise and disapproval. Some visitors objected, for instance, to the bright neon signage of *Sapientae Verbi (words of wisdom)*, *2001*, created by Jeff Chiplis and Dana Paterson at both of the cemetery's entrances. Other viewers were dazzled. (Lake View Cemetery.)

A NEW LOOK. This life-like, semi-nude female figure entitled *Timeless, 1997*, by artist Dora Natella creates a dramatic contrast with the modestly clothed Victorian statuary of the cemetery's early decades. In 1923, Lake View's trustees rejected a nude statue by a distinguished local sculptor on the grounds that it was not suitable for a cemetery. (Lake View Cemetery.)

THE WADE LAKE. Hugh Russell's arresting steel sphere, *Groundstate III, 1992,* floating on the lake behind the Wade Chapel, fitted seamlessly into the landscape, evidence of the artist's belief that the sphere is the most common universal form. (Lake View Cemetery.)

REMAINING TO CELEBRATE. Some pieces of art remained after the exhibit closed. Joyce Burstein's *The Epitaph Project* created a traditional tombstone, carved from slate. Visitors are invited to leave messages like this one with the chalk provided. (James W. Garrett IV.)

AMERICAN HEROES' DAY, 2003. On September 11, 2002, the first anniversary of the terrorists' attack on the United States in which civilians and New York safety forces died, Lake View instituted this event to honor local safety forces. "Honor Our American Heroes; Celebrate Our American Spirit" was its theme. A year later, members of fire, police, and emergency crews opened the ceremony with this procession toward the Garfield Monument. (Joseph W. Darwal.)

COMMUNITY LEADERS. Speakers at American Heroes' Day 2002 included the mayors of the three cities in which Lake View is located (from left to right, front row): Cleveland Mayor Jane Campbell; East Cleveland Mayor Emmanuel W. Onunwor, and Cleveland Heights Mayor Ed Kelley. (Laura Roberts Dempsey.)

SINGING OF HEROES. The youth choir of nearby Coventry Elementary School in Cleveland Heights provided patriotic music on the steps of the Garfield Monument on American Heroes Day, 2002. (Laura Roberts Dempsey.)

A Sign of the Times. All is not pomp and ceremony at Lake View. The cemetery continues to age, and its monuments and infrastructure often need repair. This sign warns visitors not to step onto this weakened stone balcony. (James W. Garrett IV.)

Location, Location, Location. Another sign of the times: this lighthearted advertisement for cemetery plots. Lake View continues to expand in the face of increasing competition from public and private cemeteries far distant from the city of Cleveland. (This section has since been developed.) (Laura Roberts Dempsey.)

FAITH AND HOPE REVISITED. Because the cemetery is a place for the living, they make it their own, honoring in their own ways its people and places. Here is an unsentimental, but not disrespectful comment on the Victorian figures symbolizing faith and hope. These large figures stand on an impressive pedestal, high above the ground. How someone managed to place the sunglasses on the figure to the right is anyone's guess. (Marian J. Morton.)

STUDY IN CONTRASTS. Visitors of all ages enjoy Lake View despite the solemn setting. The smiling boy and the sorrowing Victorian woman, a full century older, complement one another. (Marian J. Morton.)

REMEMBERING THE DEAD. Lake View frowns upon graveside decorations such as these brightly colored plastic balloons because they disturb the visual decorum and the manicured landscape. People leave them anyway to remember the dead on birthdays or other holidays. (Marian J. Morton.)

MESSAGE FOR WINTER. Weary of Cleveland's long winter, someone has wished it goodbye on Joyce Burstein's *The Epitaph Project*. Visitors change the messages almost daily. (Laura Roberts Dempsey.)

MESSAGE FOR "CHAPPIE." Ray Chapman, a Cleveland Indians player who died on August 17, 1920, after being hit by a pitched ball, is memorialized by this handsome Carabelli-designed monument. Faithful fans still honor Chapman by leaving baseball hats, gloves, balls, tickets to Indians games, and personal notes at this grave site. (James W. Garrett IV.)

DEATH AND LIFE AT LAKE VIEW. The thousands of individual monuments at Lake View tell the life stories of the thousands who are buried here. Together, these monuments and these lives tell the story of the city itself. In this photograph, the dramatic juxtaposition of the gravestones and the Cleveland skyline is another reminder that this place that remembers and honors death is inextricably tied to the living. The cemetery's walls and gates cannot separate it from the promises and problems of the city, for the past and present of Cleveland and Lake View are inextricably linked. So will their future be. (Laura Roberts Dempsey.)

BIBLIOGRAPHY

Cigliano, Jan. *Showplace of America: Cleveland's Euclid Avenue, 1850–1910* (Kent: Kent State University Press, 1991).

Cleveland Press.

Cleveland Plain Dealer.

Dooner, Vincetta DiRocco and Jean Marie Bossu. *Seasons of Life and Learning: Lake View Cemetery. An Educator's Handbook* (Cleveland: Lake View Cemetery Foundation, 1990).

James A. Garfield Monument at Lake View Cemetery. Cleveland, Ohio (Cleveland: Lake View Cemetery, n.d.).

Jeptha Wade Memorial Chapel (Cleveland: Lake View Cemetery Association, n.d.).

Johannesen, Eric. *Cleveland Architecture, 1876–1976.* (Cleveland: Western Reserve Historical Society, 1979).

Lake View Cemetery, Board of Trustees, Minutes, 1869–2002. Lake View Cemetery, Cleveland, OH.

Lake View Cemetery. *The Heritage*, 1986–2002.

Linden-Ward, Blanche. *Silent City on a Hill: Landscapes of Memory and Boston's Mount Auburn Cemetery* (Columbus: Ohio State University Press, 1989).

Meyer, Richard E., editor. *Ethnicity and the American Cemetery* (Bowling Green, OH: Bowling Green State University Popular Press, 1993).

Mitford, Jessica. *The American Way of Death* (New York: Simon and Schuster, 1963).

Picturesque Cleveland (Cleveland: A.C. Rogers Company. nd [circa 1901]).

Rose, William Ganson. *Cleveland: The Making of a City* (Cleveland: World Publishing, 1950).

Schuyler, David Paul. "Public Landscapes and American Urban Culture 1800–1870: Rural Cemeteries, City Parks, and Suburbs." PhD dissertation, Columbia University, 1979.

Sloane, David Charles. *The Last Great Necessity: Cemeteries in American History* (Baltimore and London: The Johns Hopkins University Press, 1991).

Tittle, Diana. *Down the Garden Path: Landscape Design and Horticulture* (Cleveland: Lake View Cemetery, 1995).

Van Tassel, David V., and John J. Grabowski, editors. *Encyclopedia of Cleveland History* (Bloomington: Indiana University Press, 1987).

Vigil, Vicki Blum. *Cleveland Cemeteries: Stones, Symbols, and Stories* (Cleveland: Gray and Company, Publishers, 1999).

Visit us at
arcadiapublishing.com

....

Printed in the USA
CPSIA information can be obtained
at www.ICGtesting.com
LVHW080945121123
763704LV00008B/162